CONVERGE
Bible Studies

IDOLATRY

Bible Studies

IDOLATRY

CURTIS ZACKERY

Abingdon Press

Nashville

IDOLATRY
CONVERGE BIBLE STUDIES

By Curtis Zackery

Library of Congress Cataloging-in-Publication Data has been requested.

ISBN: 978-1-4267-9554-1

Series Editor: Shane Raynor

14 15 16 17 18 19 20 21 22 23—10 9 8 7 6 5 4 3 2 1

Manufactured in the United States of America

CONTENTS

About the Series / 7

Introduction / 9

1: No Other Gods / 13

2: Taking Inventory / 25

3: Destroying Idols / 37

4: Restoring Hope / 51

ABOUT THE SERIES

Converge is a series of topical Bible studies based on
the Common English Bible translation. Each title in the
Converge series consists of four studies based around a
common topic or theme. *Converge* brings together a unique
group of writers from different backgrounds, traditions,
and age groups.

HOW TO USE THESE STUDIES

Converge Bible studies can be used by small groups, classes,
or individuals. Each study uses a simple format. For the
convenience of the reader, the primary Scripture passages
are included. In Insight and Ideas, the author of the study
explores each Scripture passage, going deeper into the
text and helping readers understand how the Scripture
connects with the theme of the study. Questions are
designed to encourage both personal reflection and group

conversation. Some questions may not have simple answers. That's part of what makes studying the Bible so exciting.

Although Bible passages are included with each session, study participants may find it useful to have personal Bibles on hand for referencing other Scriptures. *Converge* studies are designed for use with the Common English Bible; but they work well with any modern, reliable translation.

ONLINE EXTRAS

Converge studies are available in both print and digital formats. Each title in the series has additional components that are available online, including related blog posts and podcasts.

To access the companion materials, visit

http://www.MinistryMatters.com/Converge

Thanks for using *Converge*!

INTRODUCTION

When ministry became an idol in my life, I knew that something was terribly wrong. In the midst of doing a lot of "Christian" things, I felt extremely empty and alone. I felt as though the Lord was asking me the question, "If I were to take your role and 'position' away from you, would you still worship me with the same fervor and intensity?" My honest answer was no. I had grown extremely attached to the "how" and grown further away from the "who." It's a scary thing to realize that you've been extremely active in and around the things of God but that your affections for God have become small. I gave more to ministry than I did to Jesus.

It was extremely humbling for me to see that my *work* for God had actually become a barrier to *intimacy* with God. This led me to begin to take inventory of my life to determine the other areas that had been receiving an improper amount of affection and attention. The list was surprising—and long. I was shocked to realize how big a part of my life idolatry had become. I simply didn't want to believe that it was true. I thought to myself, *How could a guy who believes that God is God have another 'idol' that's an object of worship?*

The problem is that we have preconceived notions about idolatry and what it looks like in our lives. We've identified specific things that aren't good for us and therefore must be avoided. We've also done the same for things, people, and ideas that are OK to engage in. For the most part, we've set up self-imposed boundaries that protect us and provide justification for things that we want to remain in our life conversation.

This reminds me of a story in Scripture that describes an interaction between a lawyer and Jesus. When the lawyer stands up in Luke 10:25-29 and asks Jesus how he can inherit eternal life, Jesus responds with this question:

> "What is written in the Law? How do you interpret it?"

> [The lawyer] responded, *"You must love the Lord your God with all your heart, with all your being, with all your strength, and with all your mind, and love your neighbor as yourself."*

> Jesus said to him, "You have answered correctly. Do this and you will live."

When the lawyer hears this, his response is disheartening:

> "But he, desiring to justify himself, said to Jesus. . . ." (ESV)

His response sounds a lot like mine.

So often, the immediate response to the discovery of truth and a challenge to our character is to justify why an idol's presence is OK in our lives. I know that I can fill in the blank with numerous things that I have said to Jesus just like the lawyer did in order to explain away such areas in my life. Rather than to justify, I need to ask the honest question, "How can I submit to what God requires of me?"

I began to think about my life as a kingdom, with a large throne in the palace at the center of it—my heart. As with any kingdom, the one who is seated on the throne is the one who will determine the course of life for its subjects. The one seated on the throne will receive the affections and allegiance of its followers.

When I made an honest assessment, I realized that there were various things that had been seated on the throne of my life from time to time. The difficult and humbling truth was that Jesus was seldom seated there.

Over the years, many brilliant volumes have been penned on the subject of idolatry. It is a large idea, with many variances in the conversation. The hope for this particular study is to begin us on a journey toward understanding idolatry and its damaging effect on our connection with our savior. I think that it best for us to begin with one simple question: What or who is seated on the throne of your heart?

1

NO OTHER GODS
DEFINING AND RECOGNIZING IDOLATRY

SCRIPTURE
EXODUS 20:1-6; EXODUS 32:1-14

EXODUS 20:1-6

¹Then God spoke all these words:

²I am the LORD your God who brought you out of Egypt, out of the house of slavery.

³You must have no other gods before¹ me.

⁴Do not make an idol for yourself—no form whatsoever—of anything in the sky above or on the earth below or in the waters under the earth. ⁵Do not bow down to them or worship them, because I, the LORD your God, am a passionate God. I punish children for their parents' sins even to the third and fourth

---

1. Or *besides*

generations of those who hate me. [6]But I am loyal and gracious to the thousandth generation[2] of those who love me and keep my commandments.

EXODUS 32:1-14

[1]The people saw that Moses was taking a long time to come down from the mountain. They gathered around Aaron and said to him, "Come on! Make us gods[3] who can lead us. As for this man Moses who brought us up out of the land of Egypt, we don't have a clue what has happened to him."

[2]Aaron said to them, "All right, take out the gold rings from the ears of your wives, your sons, and your daughters, and bring them to me." [3]So all the people took out the gold rings from their ears and brought them to Aaron. [4]He collected them and tied them up in a cloth.[4] Then he made a metal image of a bull calf, and the people declared, "These are your gods, Israel, who brought you up out of the land of Egypt!"

[5]When Aaron saw this, he built an altar in front of the calf. Then Aaron announced, "Tomorrow will be a festival to the LORD!" [6]They got up early the next day and offered up entirely burned offerings and brought well-being sacrifices. The people sat down to eat and drink and then got up to celebrate.

---

2. Or to thousands
3. Or a god
4. Or formed them into a mold or engraved them with a stylus

[7]The LORD spoke to Moses: "Hurry up and go down! Your people, whom you brought up out of the land of Egypt, are ruining everything! [8]They've already abandoned the path that I commanded. They have made a metal bull calf for themselves. They've bowed down to it and offered sacrifices to it and declared, 'These are your gods, Israel, who brought you up out of the land of Egypt!' " [9]The LORD said to Moses, "I've been watching these people, and I've seen how stubborn they are. [10]Now leave me alone! Let my fury burn and devour them. Then I'll make a great nation out of you."

[11]But Moses pleaded with the LORD his God, "LORD, why does your fury burn against your own people, whom you brought out of the land of Egypt with great power and amazing force? [12]Why should the Egyptians say, 'He had an evil plan to take the people out and kill them in the mountains and so wipe them off the earth'? Calm down your fierce anger. Change your mind about doing terrible things to your own people. [13]Remember Abraham, Isaac, and Israel, your servants, whom you yourself promised, 'I'll make your descendants as many as the stars in the sky. And I've promised to give your descendants this whole land to possess for all time.'" [14]Then the LORD changed his mind about the terrible things he said he would do to his people.

INSIGHT AND IDEAS

Idolatry is one of the most dangerous areas of sin that we can experience in our lives. The danger lies in all of the nuances that are attached to it. Although, in our minds, we usually identify them as bad, idols might not always be inherently "bad" things. This is where the issue of idolatry can become a bit tricky.

Because of the complexity attached to idolatry, it isn't often that we delve into the subject as we pursue Jesus. The moment we begin to examine what this issue means for us, we become susceptible to the exposure of our own idols. And when idols find a comfortable place in our lives, they become very difficult to uproot.

Not many people would personally identify with the word *idol*. We might admit that there are things in our lives that take up much of our time and attention. We might even identify someone or something that consumes most of our affections. But most of us would not go as far as to call those things idols. When we hear the word *idol,* we recount Bible stories that we've heard of groups of people who would build a golden calf or some other object of worship and dedicate their lives to serving and worshipping it. Many of our thoughts about idols are so far-fetched that we could never see ourselves associating with idolatry in any fashion. But if we examine the definition of *idol,* I think that many of us would be surprised.

The American Heritage Dictionary[5] defines an *idol* as "an image used as an object of worship; a false god." If we stop there, it would be easy for a lot of us to disassociate from idols. The second definition, however, identifies an idol as "one that is adored, often blindly or excessively." *Idolatry*, the worship of idols, is defined as "blind or excessive devotion to something." Practically everyone can identify with this definition.

Martin Luther said, "Whatever your heart clings to and confides in, that is really your God."[6] This is the essence of understanding idolatry. It's all about where our hearts reside. It's easy for us to talk about the things that are ultimately important to us, but it's how we respond in our hearts that truly matters.

IT'S ALL ABOUT OUR AFFECTIONS

Everyone has affection for something. It doesn't take a whole lot of convincing for us to arrive at this fact. The word *affection* can be described by other words, such as *fondness, love, devotion, endearment*, and *attachment*. I can guarantee that there is something present in your life that, if it were removed, would devastate you. This something or someone may be a very good and beautiful thing. On the other hand, it may be some sort of vice or destructive behavior. Whatever you're attached to could be as simple as your cell phone or as significant as a relationship with a loved one.

---

5. *The American Heritage Dictionary of the English Language, Fifth Edition* (Houghton Mifflin Harcourt, 2014). *http://ahdictionary.com*. Accessed 5 May 2014.
6. From *Luther's Large Catechism*, edited by J.N. Lenker (The Luther Press, 1908); page 44.

There's nothing wrong with having affections. This is, indeed, the way that God created us. We are worshippers by design. Since we all have affection, the question becomes what do we have affection for? If we're honest with ourselves, it's not very difficult to identify the places where our affections lie.

When investigating the effects of a particular sin issue and the prospective remedies in our lives, we should begin with what the Bible says about the subject.

THE BIBLE ON IDOLATRY

It's evident throughout Scripture that idolatry is a big deal. From the very beginning, humanity was intended to worship and to be in relationship with God with no barriers. We were, in fact, created to give our affections to the God who created us. But the Bible shows us that there are clear consequences of misplaced affection or worship.

In the Old Testament, we see that when the Law was handed down to Moses in the Ten Commandments that God was explicit about where our worship was intended to go: "You must have no other gods before me. Do not make an idol for yourself—no form whatsoever—of anything in the sky above or on the earth below or in the waters under the earth" (Exodus 20:3-4).

We also see the Lord's response when the people Moses was leading went against this instruction:

The Lord spoke to Moses: "Hurry up and go down! Your
people, whom you brought up out of the land of Egypt, are
ruining everything! They've already abandoned the path that I
commanded. They have made a metal bull calf for themselves.
They've bowed down to it and offered sacrifices to it and
declared, 'These are your gods, Israel, who brought you up out
of the land of Egypt!'" (Exodus 32:7-8)

The Book of Deuteronomy has some very pointed
words concerning idolatry, including these: "You must
follow the Lord your God alone! Revere him! Follow his
commandments! Obey his voice! Worship him! Cling to
him—no other!" (Deuteronomy 13:4).

The Bible is very clear with humanity about God's position
in our lives. When we refer to God as a "jealous God," this
is what we mean. There is to be nothing that will receive
the praise that is intended for God alone. Many of us look
at this statement and feel that it doesn't sound right to
say that God is "jealous." The difference between jealousy
in terms of humans and in terms of God is simple. God
wants all of our affection because God is the only one who
deserves it.

The New Testament is filled with further examples of the
importance of living a life that is unencumbered by idols.
In his first letter to the Thessalonians, Paul gives us a clear
perspective on idolatry and the position that God should
hold in our lives:

People tell us about what sort of welcome we had from you and how you turned to God from idols. As a result, you are serving the living and true God, and you are waiting for his Son from heaven. His Son is Jesus, who is the one he raised from the dead and who is the one who will rescue us from the coming wrath. (1 Thessalonians 1:9-10)

Here we see that it's possible to be freed from the captivity of idolatry. While it's important for us to understand that idols have a devastating impact on our lives, it's also important to know that we can be redeemed!

WHAT DOES THIS MEAN FOR US?

John Calvin once said, "Every one of us is, even from his mother's womb, expert in inventing idols."[7] I've also heard it simply stated that our hearts are "idol factories." Because we are worshippers by nature, and because we are continually pursuing satisfaction, it's easy to find things that we give ourselves to. This, in turn, creates a dynamic in which the worship that was intended for God goes toward other things.

If a quarterback on a football team drops back to throw a pass to the intended receiver and a player from the defense intercepts the pass, there's an obvious problem. What was intended to go to a particular recipient now has been stolen. What was meant to go in one direction is now headed in the other. When idols are present in our lives,

---

7. *Calvin's Commentaries: Acts 28; http://biblehub.com/commentaries/calvin/acts/28.htm.* Accessed 5 May 2014.

they intercept the worship that is intended for the Living God who created us.

This is a very simplified analogy, but it certainly sums up the idea. When we're talking about football, the obvious remedy is to overcome the obstacles to completing the pass. We want to avoid the players on the other team who can steal the ball and keep us from going in the direction that we're supposed to be going. When it comes to idolatry, we need to apply the same principle.

THROWING OFF EXTRA BAGGAGE

There is a passage in Hebrews that sums up what our approach should be in dealing with idols:

> So then let's also run the race that is laid out in front of us, since we have such a great cloud of witnesses surrounding us. Let's throw off any extra baggage, get rid of the sin that trips us up, and fix our eyes on Jesus, faith's pioneer and perfecter. He endured the cross, ignoring the shame, for the sake of the joy that was laid out in front of him, and sat down at the right side of God's throne. (Hebrews 12:1-2)

For us to "throw off any extra baggage" and "get rid of the sin that trips us up," we have to do some work to identify what these things are. It's important for us to take note how the writer addresses two separate issues in this statement. Often, we immediately move to the "sin that trips us up" part of the verse when dealing with idolatry because these areas are usually more readily identifiable.

If I know that there is some sort of persistent sin issue or addiction that I am battling, I'm fully aware that this thing is stealing affections from a God who would have no dealings with them.

Idolatry becomes a bit trickier when we start trying to figure out what might be the "extra baggage" in our lives. These are the things, people, or interests that, although may be good things, can be a hindrance to us moving forward in our relationship with the Lord. The term "extra baggage" leads us to try to determine what is expendable.

When we're taking a trip and have too much baggage, we have to try to see what we can unpack and leave behind so it won't weigh us down as we go. We must open up our bags to see what's in there that isn't vital to the trip and can be left behind. Some of the things that we recognize as items that we might not need for the trip are still very important. They just might not be helpful when we're trying to get to where we're trying to go.

I think its easy for us to see the parallel when it comes to identifying idols in our lives that might be either holding us back or tripping us up. It's extremely important that we figure out what these things are so we can either put them in their proper place or eliminate them from our lives altogether.

QUESTIONS

1. Why was God so concerned about "other gods" (Exodus 20:3)?

2. Why would God punish children and grandchildren for their parents' and grandparents' sins (Exodus 20:5)?

3. What is significant about the numbers of generations listed in Exodus 20:5-6? Why are these numbers different? What might this tell us about God?

4. Why did the people ask Aaron to make idols for them? Why were the people so impatient? Why, do you think, did Aaron agree to do it (Exodus 32:1-2)?

5. Why did Aaron invoke the name of the Lord (Yahweh) after making a calf and an altar (Exodus 32:5)?

6. Why does God refer to the Israelites as "your people" when telling Moses about the idolatry going on at the foot of Mount Sinai (Exodus 32:7)?

7. Why did the calf make God so angry (Exodus 32:8)? How does God feel about idolatry today? What forms does idolatry take in the twenty-first century?

8. What did Moses say to persuade God not to destroy the Israelites?

9. Exodus 32:14 says, "The Lord changed his mind about the terrible things he said he would do to his people." What brought about this change? Why might some people find this action theologically perplexing?

10. How do we know when to put an idol in its proper place and when to eliminate it from our lives altogether?

2

TAKING INVENTORY
IDENTIFYING OUR IDOLS

SCRIPTURE
ROMANS 1:18-25; DEUTERONOMY 13:1-4

ROMANS 1:18-25

[18]God's wrath is being revealed from heaven against all the ungodly behavior and the injustice of human beings who silence the truth with injustice. [19]This is because what is known about God should be plain to them because God made it plain to them. [20]Ever since the creation of the world, God's invisible qualities—God's eternal power and divine nature—have been clearly seen, because they are understood through the things God has made. So humans are without excuse. [21]Although they knew God, they didn't honor God as God or thank him. Instead, their reasoning became pointless, and their foolish hearts were darkened. [22]While they were claiming to be wise, they made fools of themselves. [23]They exchanged the glory of the immortal God for images that

look like mortal humans: birds, animals, and reptiles. ²⁴So God abandoned them to their hearts' desires, which led to the moral corruption of degrading their own bodies with each other. ²⁵They traded God's truth for a lie, and they worshipped and served the creation instead of the creator, who is blessed forever. Amen.

DEUTERONOMY 13:1-4

¹Now if a prophet or a dream interpreter appears among you and performs a sign or wonder for you, ²and the sign or wonder that was spoken actually occurs; if he says: "Come on! We should follow other gods"—ones you haven't experienced—"and we should worship them," ³you must not listen to that prophet's or dream interpreter's words, because the Lord your God is testing you to see if you love the Lord your God with all your mind and all your being. ⁴You must follow the Lord your God alone! Revere him! Follow his commandments! Obey his voice! Worship him! Cling to him—no other!

INSIGHT AND IDEAS

We have already defined *idols* as interrupters or thieves of worship. This is significant because idolatry disrupts the very purpose God had for us from the beginning: We were created to be in relationship with and to worship God forever. In Isaiah 43:7, God talks about those "whom I created for my glory." In Ephesians 1:6, Paul discusses how we are to live "to honor [God's] glorious grace that he has given to us freely." In Psalm 50:23, we see a very clear picture of the significance of our worship of God: "The one who offers a sacrifice of thanksgiving is the one who honors me. And it is to the one who charts the correct path that I will show divine salvation."

When we worship God, it brings glory to the one who is intended to receive glory. We give true honor where honor is due. And when we're properly aligned in our worship, it benefits us as well. As we lift up the name of Jesus, worship helps us center and focus on the most important things. Peace and rest come as a result of directing our affections where they were intended to go. We've already determined that for most of us, there are probably areas that are intercepting the worship that is intended for God. Before we move forward, we have to figure out what those things are in our lives.

CREATURE OVER CREATOR

Author and pastor Timothy Keller said, "If anything becomes more fundamental than God to your happiness, meaning in life, and identity, then it is an idol."[1] This is a clear description of the things that we give our affections to that have taken away from our worship and satisfaction in the Lord. This is not a new issue. Since sin entered the world, humanity has been attempting to satisfy an eternal longing with temporal things that aren't designed to satisfy us.

---

1. From *Counterfeit Gods: The Empty Promises of Money, Sex, and Power, and the Only Hope that Matters,* by Timothy Keller (Penguin, 2009); page xix.

> They exchanged the glory of the immortal God for images that look like mortal humans: birds, animals, and reptiles. So God abandoned them to their hearts' desires, which led to the moral corruption of degrading their own bodies with each other. They traded God's truth for a lie, and they worshipped and served the creation instead of the creator, who is blessed forever. Amen. (Romans 1:23-25)

When I read this passage in Romans, I can't help but think that it sounds a lot like our culture. What Paul is saying here is that there were people who were worshipping the stuff the creator made rather than the creator of all of the stuff.

The tricky thing is trying to identify what those things are in our lives. What we must realize is that even though something is a good thing, we might still be giving it an improper place. If this is the case, it may be stealing the worship intended for God and assuming too much of our affection. We need honesty, courage, and help to identify what our idols are.

HONESTY, COURAGE, AND HELP

When it comes to identifying our idols, the biggest barrier is usually us. We get in our own way because of our lack of willingness to admit the areas where our affections are misplaced. Remember, the things or people that are receiving the worship intended for God might not be inherently bad things. However, this is where we can fall into the rhythm of justification.

We can't properly address the areas that are causing us to be distracted unless we are honest with ourselves about them. In Hebrews, we receive some important instruction about how to move forward in our pursuit of Christ:

> So then let's also run the race that is laid out in front of us, since we have such a great cloud of witnesses surrounding us. Let's throw off any extra baggage, get rid of the sin that trips us up, and fix our eyes on Jesus, faith's pioneer and perfecter. He endured the cross, ignoring the shame, for the sake of the joy that was laid out in front of him, and sat down at the right side of God's throne. (Hebrews 12:1-2)

It takes courage for us to move forward in identifying our idols. When we begin to confront the areas that we recognize as having an improper place in our lives, we engage in a fight that is spiritually, emotionally, and sometimes physically taxing. Knowing whether to reorder or release things that have become idols can be difficult, and fear is one of the biggest deterrents to doing the hard work of unearthing things that we know are causing us difficulties. It is extremely important for us to be honest and to do some self-assessment. There are places in our hearts that only we know exist and only we can diagnose as barriers to worship. It takes courage to look at these things straight on and engage in the hard work of adjustment.

Sometimes we also need someone who will help us identify the idols that we can't see for ourselves. Many of us have allowed certain idols to be a part of our lives for so long that we've become extremely accustomed to their being there. We've grown comfortable with a mode of living that allows us to justify certain actions or attitudes that may be worship barriers. When we have idols that may be in our blind spots, it helps to have people in our lives who will lovingly tell us the truth.

AN IDOL DISCOVERY

For a period of time in my life, technology became a bit of an idol for me. This wasn't an easy discovery for me to face. I was completely into gadgets and was constantly looking toward what the next new thing would be. Now when I say this, many people push back because technology is such an everyday part of our lives. But this is a classic indicator of an idol.

Suppose I were to say that a "god" was constantly occupying my thoughts, that I gave a lot of money toward connecting with it, and that most of my time was spent interacting with it. Other people would easily recognize this as an idol. The problem is that we allow ourselves to soften the reality of idolatry, based upon what our culture deems acceptable. This occurs often. Our personal connection with Christ is then determined by public expectation.

Consider what Paul wrote in 1 Corinthians 6:12: "I have the freedom to do anything, but not everything is helpful. I have the freedom to do anything, but I won't be controlled by anything." Even a good thing can become bad if we get our priorities out of order.

Once we understand the significance of idolatry and idols and their effects on our worship, we need to do the hard and important work of identifying what they are in our own lives:

Lᴏʀᴅ, you are my strength and my stronghold; you are my refuge in time of trouble. The nations will flock to you from the ends of the earth, and they will say: "Our ancestors have inherited utter lies, things that are hollow and useless." Can humans make their own gods? If so, they are not gods at all! (Jeremiah 16:19-20)

GIFTS AND THE GIVER

I had an interesting childhood, one where I didn't get to spend much time with my extended family. I don't remember much from growing up, but I do remember a few scattered times of visiting my grandparents. Interestingly enough, when I think back to the times that we'd go visit them, there's only one vivid thing that I can recall: the gifts that I received. (I know that's very selfish and simple; but I have to be honest, right?)

I always knew that when I went to their house, there would be some sort of gift for me. It might be as simple as some candy, a little toy, or some pocket change; but as a little kid, I would love it. I began to expect that there would be some sort of transaction that would happen every time I arrived. The expectation of these arrival gifts or treats always made me want to go and visit. I'd never really spend time with the giver of the gifts; I'd just enjoy the gifts.

Later on, I thought back to that time. I remembered that when my grandfather passed away, I didn't have a very strong emotional response. I realized that I didn't really know my grandfather very well. As a matter of fact, I have more memories about the types of things that he would give me than I actually have about him. I don't remember getting to know my grandfather. I don't remember hearing him tell me stories or talking about the things that he loved.

Reflecting on this season helped me realize that this very idea connected to my spiritual life. It dawned on me that this was the same way that I approached my relationship with Jesus. I cared more about the gifts than I did about the one who gave me the gifts. I realized that there was no intimacy shared in connection with Christ. All of my association was through what I hoped Christ would give me or do for me.

IDOL INDICATORS: OUR THOUGHTS

In my experience, there are three key areas that, if assessed honestly, can help point to the existence of idols in our lives. These areas are our thoughts, our time, and our treasure. These are three big indicators to help us figure out where we're placing our affection. Matthew 22:37 says, "*You must love the Lord your God with all your heart, with all your being,* and with all your mind." This is how we should be living our lives. If there are things present that are barriers to this occurring, they are idols.

Our minds go to the places where our affections lie. More plainly said, we think about the things we care about. If we actually stop and assess the things that we spend most of the day thinking about, it's not hard to figure out where our affections really lie. Many of us, when pressed, would say that God is the most important thing in our lives. But can we honestly say that our thoughts would bear out this statement?

It's difficult to keep track of our thoughts, since our minds are processing continually throughout the day. I've found it helpful to take some quiet time of reflection at the end of my day to think about the general places my thoughts have traveled and to write down my discovery.

OUR TIME

What do we spend our time doing from day to day? Our answer to this question will show us what we really care about. We can say that something is important, but actions speak louder than words. Once I was challenged in a class to keep a personal log of how I spent each hour for an entire week. The results were quite revealing. Anyone could take a quick glance at this log and see the things that were most important to me. The ways that I spent my time reflected where my affections and priorities were.

It's a good idea to regularly assess where we're spending our time and see how that aligns with a lifestyle that calls for us to worship the Lord with all of our heart.

OUR TREASURE

There's a reason that there are hundreds of Scriptures that talk about money and stewardship. Money is an important issue in our lives, and what we do with our money is a clear reflection of the things that are in our hearts.

If you want to see where your affections really are, take some time and determine your monthly spending. Don't just look ahead to the ways that you desire to spend your money, but take a hard look back at the ways that you've been spending your money over the past few months. If you need to, maybe even take a look at a few of your old bank statements.

All of these indicators can go a long way toward helping us identify where we are feeding our idols. But naming our idols is one thing; dealing with them is something else entirely. We'll explore that in the next session.

QUESTIONS

1. What is injustice? How does injustice silence the truth (Romans 1:18)?

2. How are God's invisible qualities "clearly seen" (Romans 1:20)? What implications does this verse have for those who don't acknowledge God?

3. What does it mean to honor God as God? How is it possible to know God but not honor God (Romans 1:21)?

4. Describe a "darkened heart" (Romans 1:21). How does someone avoid a darkened heart (Romans 1:22)?

5. Why do people seem to want to follow gods they can see (Romans 1:24)?

6. What are ways people trade God's truth for lies (Romans 1:25)? How do we recognize when we're the ones doing this?

7. What does a false prophet look like today (Deuteronomy 13:1)?

8. How does our culture encourage following other gods (Deuteronomy 13:2)?

9. Does God test believers today? What is the difference between testing and temptation (Deuteronomy 13:3)?

10. Why is the message of Deuteronomy 13:4 so emphatic?

11. Why is it so important to enlist the help of others when identifying our own idols?

3

DESTROYING IDOLS
CHANGING OUR HEARTS AND LIVES

SCRIPTURE
COLOSSIANS 3:1-17; GENESIS 22:6-14

COLOSSIANS 3:1-17

¹Therefore, if you were raised with Christ, look for the things that are above where Christ is sitting at God's right side. ²Think about the things above and not things on earth. ³You died, and your life is hidden with Christ in God. ⁴When Christ, who is your life, is revealed, then you also will be revealed with him in glory.

⁵So put to death the parts of your life that belong to the earth, such as sexual immorality, moral corruption, lust, evil desire, and greed (which is idolatry). ⁶The wrath of God is coming upon disobedient people because of these things. ⁷You used to live this way, when you were alive to these things. ⁸But now set aside these things, such as anger, rage, malice, slander, and obscene

language. [9]Don't lie to each other. Take off the old human nature with its practices [10]and put on the new nature, which is renewed in knowledge by conforming to the image of the one who created it. [11]In this image there is neither Greek nor Jew, circumcised nor uncircumcised, barbarian, Scythian, slave nor free, but Christ is all things and in all people.

[12]Therefore, as God's choice, holy and loved, put on compassion, kindness, humility, gentleness, and patience. [13]Be tolerant with each other and, if someone has a complaint against anyone, forgive each other. As the Lord forgave you, so also forgive each other. [14]And over all these things put on love, which is the perfect bond of unity. [15]The peace of Christ must control your hearts—a peace into which you were called in one body. And be thankful people. [16]The word of Christ must live in you richly. Teach and warn each other with all wisdom by singing psalms, hymns, and spiritual songs. Sing to God with gratitude in your hearts. [17]Whatever you do, whether in speech or action, do it all in the name of the Lord Jesus and give thanks to God the Father through him.

GENESIS 22:6-14

[6]Abraham took the wood for the entirely burned offering and laid it on his son Isaac. He took the fire and the knife in his hand, and the two of them walked on together. [7]Isaac said to his father Abraham, "My father?"

Abraham said, "I'm here, my son."

Isaac said, "Here is the fire and the wood, but where is the lamb for the entirely burned offering?"

[8]Abraham said, "The lamb for the entirely burned offering? God will see to it,[1] my son." The two of them walked on together.

[9]They arrived at the place God had described to him. Abraham built an altar there and arranged the wood on it. He tied up his son Isaac and laid him on the altar on top of the wood. [10]Then Abraham stretched out his hand and took the knife to kill his son as a sacrifice. [11]But the LORD's messenger called out to Abraham from heaven, "Abraham? Abraham?"

Abraham said, "I'm here."

[12]The messenger said, "Don't stretch out your hand against the young man, and don't do anything to him. I now know that you revere God and didn't hold back your son, your only son, from me." [13]Abraham looked up and saw a single ram caught by its horns in the dense underbrush. Abraham went over, took the ram, and offered it as an entirely burned offering instead of his son. [14]Abraham named that place "the LORD sees."[2] That is the reason people today say, "On this mountain the LORD is seen.

---

1. Or God will see; or God will provide
2. Or the LORD is seen; or the LORD provides

INSIGHT AND IDEAS

When we recognize that there's an issue that is blocking our exclusive worship of God, we need to do all that we can to get rid of it. It all boils down to one thing: Idols hinder our connection with the God who deserves all of our affection, and they must be removed. The obvious question, then, is how do we do it?

MORE THAN WILLPOWER

First we must realize that we're making a huge mistake if we try to assume the lion's share of responsibility when we attempt to destroy our idols. Some of us seem to believe that our strong will and hard work will help us withstand the temptations of idolatry, but author and pastor J. Heinrich Arnold disagreed with such a notion when he wrote: "As long as we try to conquer evil by sheer willpower, evil will get the better of us."[3]

Our desire to remove idols from our lives sometimes leads us toward attempting to make it happen under our own strength. And just as often as we attempt it on our own, we fail.

The cycle of removing idols and falling back into aligning our affections with them is a dance many of us do. The times that we fail create guilt and shame that cause us to be discouraged and to believe that the proper alignment

---

3. From *Freedom From Sinful Thoughts*, by J. Heinrich Arnold, (Plough Publishing House, 2007); page 15.

of our worship isn't even possible. That's when we realize that destroying idolatry in our lives isn't simply a matter of procedure. It goes much deeper.

IT STARTS WITH THE HEART

For us to see true change, it must begin in our hearts. I remember a season in my life when I began to understand the significance of a life connected to Christ. I realized that one of the barriers to my worship of God was my love for and collection of music. Philippians 4:8 tells us that "if anything is excellent and if anything is admirable, focus your thoughts on these things: all that is true, all that is holy, all that is just, all that is pure, all that is lovely, and all that is worthy of praise." The problem was that some of the themes and ideas in the music I was listening to were distracting me and causing me to dwell on things that were *not* pure and lovely.

So I decided to make a strong move toward removing this barrier to worship. I gathered all of my CDs (remember what those are?) and threw them away. I just knew that if I got rid off all of the music, I wouldn't position myself to be tempted again. But I was only partly right. Because if the temptation arose to invest most of my time into music again, all I needed to do was go back out and buy some more music. As a matter of fact, I could just borrow it from my friends. You see, I needed my desires to change first. It all starts with the heart.

ABRAHAM, SARAH, AND ISAAC

One of the most notable examples from the Bible that deals with the issue of idolatry is found in the Book of Genesis. It's the story of Abraham and his son Isaac. First, a little bit of backstory: God promises Abraham that he will be the father of a great nation. The one big issue with this is that Abraham and his wife Sarah are already old and are childless. It would take a miracle for them to be able to conceive a son naturally.

Over time, Abraham and Sarah begin to grow impatient waiting for the fulfillment of the Lord's promise. So they decide to take matters into their own hands and have Abraham father a child with one of Sarah's maidservants. Although this union results in a son, it isn't the way that God has intended for the promise to be fulfilled. Still, despite the huge error and disobedience on Abraham's part, God returns to him and fulfills the original promise.

Once Isaac is born, Abraham and Sarah are overjoyed that they have been able to have a child together. Isaac is their prized son; he is extremely important to Abraham.

It's at this point that Abraham's affections are tested. God tells Abraham to take Isaac and sacrifice him as a burnt offering. What a scary and daunting command! What we see in response, though, is an obedient Abraham leading Isaac to the place God instructed him to go do this. Later in the story, we learn that just as the sacrifice is about to be made, God sends a ram as a substitute so that Isaac is spared.

Abraham clearly passed this test of faith. He believed that God knew what was best, even to the point of sacrificing his son.

The question we might ask here is, "How could Abraham actually do it?" We see that he had obviously wavered in faith earlier because, rather than waiting for the fulfillment of God's promise, Abraham took matters into his own hands to have a son. But now, when God asks him to sacrifice the promised Isaac, whom he and Sarah dearly love, Abraham is completely obedient. He's able to lay down his "idol" in this situation because he's had a heart change. He has clearly learned a lesson about God's trustworthiness and sovereignty.

Because Abraham trusted God, he was able to lay down something of great importance to him.

REPENTANCE

Once we've identified the idols in our lives and we realize that we need to properly align our worship, a significant step toward destroying our idols is *repentance*. The *American Heritage Dictionary* says that to repent is "to feel remorse, contrition, or self-reproach for what one has done or failed to do; be contrite."[4] I've also heard it said that to repent is to stop going in one direction, turn, and go in the other direction. It may seem like it's a an elementary truth, but the reality is we rarely live it out. Often we're lulled to sleep and continue on in our sin by justifying our idols.

4. *The American Heritage Dictionary of the English Language, Fifth Edition,* (Houghton Mifflin Harcourt, 2014). *http://ahdictionary.com.* Accessed 5 May 2014.

But there's another perspective on repentance that assists us in this conversation. If a child realizes that he or she is going in the wrong direction and understands that he or she has done wrong by the father, the child will stop and turn (repent). The child will then assume a posture that will allow the father to pick him or her up. In the father's arms, there is comfort and safety and no need to stray away.

As *we* repent of our idolatry, we need to allow the Father to pick us up and minister to the areas that are hurting.

WHO IS THE SAVIOR?

When ridding ourselves of idols, we must have a firm understanding of who actually does the redeeming. Pastor and author A. W. Tozer wrote about this idea in his book *Man, The Dwelling Place of God*:

> Grace will save a man but it will not save him and his idol. The blood of Christ will shield the penitent sinner alone, but never the sinner and his idol. Faith will justify the sinner, but it will never justify the sinner and his sin.[5]

God is our redeemer and king— the one who provides salvation and rescue from the captivity of the idols that steal our worship. Our God will never justify the idolatry or worship of any "god" or thing that comes between us.

5. From *Man, the Dwelling Place of God: What It Means to Have Christ Living in You*, by A.W. Tozer, (Wing Spread Publishers, 1996); *https://books.google.com/books?isbn=1621546659*. Accessed 5 May 2014.

A song written by John Mark McMillan called "How He Loves" speaks about God's heart for us. The first line says, "He is jealous for me." In our humanity, a lot of us look at this statement and think, "Jealousy is a bad thing, isn't it?" But as an attribute of God, jealousy is a *wonderful* thing. We actually want to have a God who is "jealous" for us, because God is eternal and perfect and knows that our hearts are given over to things that do not satisfy. God's jealousy for our affections comes from a perfect knowledge that no other source will fulfill the longings we're chasing.

A right perspective of the Savior allows for idols to meet their destruction.

LAY IT DOWN

Earlier we discussed the futility of simply getting rid of the things that are causing us to stumble into idolatry without first experiencing a heart change. That said, it's still important for us to lay our idols down. In 1 Corinthians 10:14-15, Paul is clear in his advice on the proper response to idols: "So then, my dear friends, run away from the worship of false gods! I'm talking to you like you are sensible people. Think about what I'm saying." I love that he makes it so plain, essentially saying that he expects sensible people to understand such a simple and important truth.

When we experience a heart change, which can happen only through a connection with the living God, we are able to understand the proper placement of our affections. Our repentance may have us walking in a different direction, but the temptation that is connected to our fleshly desire remains. In Galatians 5, Paul reminds that we've been set free for freedom's sake and that we must not return to the bondage of slavery. Then he goes on to outline the struggle that followers of Jesus will experience for the rest of their earthly lives. Galatians 5:16-17 tells us:

> I say be guided by the Spirit and you won't carry out your selfish desires. A person's selfish desires are set against the Spirit, and the Spirit is set against one's selfish desires. They are opposed to each other, so you shouldn't do whatever you want to do.

This is key when it comes to idolatry. Because of our flesh, the desire to allow an idol to sneak back into a position in front of God is very real. This is why it is important to "run away" as Paul instructed us and to cast down idols.

In Hebrews 12:1-2, we see a great reminder of this:

> So then let's also run the race that is laid out in front of us, since we have such a great cloud of witnesses surrounding us. Let's throw off any extra baggage, get rid of the sin that trips us up, and fix our eyes on Jesus, faith's pioneer and perfecter. He endured the cross, ignoring the shame, for the sake of the joy that was laid out in front of him, and sat down at the right side of God's throne.

Right before this, in Hebrews 11, the writer lists examples of how faith endured through hope in God in the lives of many individuals. The reader is then challenged to run this same race, in faith. The warning in this verse makes sense once we connect it to the imagery of running. We wouldn't want anything to weigh us down if we were trying to run in a race, and we'd certainly want to make sure that we didn't trip.

Even if we've repented and understood that Christ is our savior, there are likely things in our lives that could still easily trip us up and cause us to fall back into the pattern of idolatry. There might also be things, issues, or people that weigh us down in the pursuit of Jesus and create unnecessary hindrances to our relationship with him.

As difficult as the prospect is, if we want to destroy idolatry in our lives, we may need to make some serious life adjustments to ensure that we are running the race well.

QUESTIONS

1. What are the "things above" Paul is telling us to think about (Colossians 3:2)? What does this verse mean when it tells us not to think about things on earth? In what ways might this verse be misunderstood?

2. When will Christ be revealed (Colossians 3:4)? How will this affect those who believe in him?

3. How do we "put to death" our old, sinful ways of life (Colossians 3:5)? Why does this verse equate greed with idolatry?

4. What does it mean to "take off the old human nature" and "put on the new nature" (Colossians 3:9-10)? How do we do this?

5. What happens when the peace of Christ isn't controlling our hearts (Colossians 3:15)?

6. What can we do to ensure that the word of Christ lives in us richly (Colossians 3:16)? Why is this so important?

7. What is the significance of Abraham's response to Isaac in Genesis 22:8?

8. Did God need to test Abraham to know what the outcome of this story would be? Why, or why not?

9. What can we learn from the story of Abraham and Isaac that can help us as we fight idolatry in our own lives?

10. What role does repentance play in our battle against idolatry?

11. What role does the Holy Spirit play in keeping us away from idols?

4

RESTORING HOPE
LIVING LIFE AS AN OVERCOMER

SCRIPTURE
HEBREWS 4:1-16

[1]Therefore, since the promise that we can enter into rest is still open, let's be careful so that none of you will appear to miss it. [2]We also had the good news preached to us, just as the Israelites did. However, the message they heard didn't help them because they weren't united in faith with the ones who listened to it. [3]We who have faith are entering the rest. As God said,

And because of my anger I swore:
"They will never enter into my rest!"[1]

And yet God's works were completed at the foundation of the world. [4]Then somewhere he said this about the seventh day of

---

1. Psalm 95:11

creation: *God rested on the seventh day from all his works.*[2] [5]But again, in the passage above, God said, *They will never enter my rest!*[3] [6]Therefore, it's left open for some to enter it, and the ones who had the good news preached to them before didn't enter because of disobedience. [7]Just as it says in the passage above, God designates a certain day as "today," when he says through David much later,

Today, if you hear his voice,

don't have stubborn hearts.[4]

[8]If Joshua gave the Israelites rest, God wouldn't have spoken about another day later on. [9]So you see that a sabbath rest is left open for God's people. [10]The one who entered God's rest also rested from his works, just as God rested from his own.

[11]Therefore, let's make every effort to enter that rest so that no one will fall by following the same example of disobedience, [12]because God's word is living, active, and sharper than any two-edged sword. It penetrates to the point that it separates the soul from the spirit and the joints from the marrow. It's able to judge the heart's thoughts and intentions. [13]No creature is hidden from it, but rather everything is naked and exposed to the eyes of the one to whom we have to give an answer.

[14]Also, let's hold on to the confession since we have a great high priest who passed through the heavens, who is Jesus, God's Son;

---

2. Genesis 2:2
3. Psalm 95:11
4. Psalm 95:7-8

[15]because we don't have a high priest who can't sympathize with our weaknesses but instead one who was tempted in every way that we are, except without sin.

[16]Finally, let's draw near to the throne of favor with confidence so that we can receive mercy and find grace when we need help.

INSIGHT AND IDEAS

Identifying and destroying idols is a humbling process. The weight of the reality that our hearts are given over to things other than God can create feelings of guilt and shame. We may begin to feel that even though God's affections for us are great, we don't deserve God's love and forgiveness. The most amazing bit of news that we can receive is that God won't leave us in our desperation and shame. The gospel is the ultimate remedy for these feelings.

The words of Paul have guided us through most of this journey, and they speak to this issue as well. After sharing his feelings of being a "miserable human being" (Romans 7:24), and explaining that grace is available only through the work of Jesus (having nothing to do with our actions), Paul writes, "So now there isn't any condemnation for those who are in Christ Jesus" (Romans 8:1).

We have an opportunity to move forward with confidence as children of God. Scripture instructs us, "Let us then with confidence draw near to the throne of grace, that we may receive mercy and find grace to help in time of need" (Hebrews 4:16, ESV). We go forward with confidence because it's not our past that's on display but the righteousness of Christ, which can come only from him. In Christ, we are clothed with righteousness. He puts it on us, like a cloak. We proceed with boldness, because it's not our work that is accounted for; it is the work of Christ.

STEPS TOWARD RESTORATION

In Deuteronomy 4:29 and Jeremiah 29:13, we see an important encouragement and challenge for those who are seeking the Lord. According to Deuteronomy, "you will find him if you seek him with all your heart and with all your being" (4:29) and in Jeremiah, God says, "When you search for me, yes, search for me with all your heart, you will find me" (29:13).

I've heard it said many times that wherever you see it in the Bible, the word *all* means all. When there are no hidden places in our hearts and we're not withholding any area of our lives from the Lord, we're able to connect through faith. Once we lay down our idols, we're ready to really engage with God.

Although this truth resonates with many of us, the actual process can seem overwhelming. The temptation to return to the idols that once tripped us up can seem too alluring to resist. And sometimes it's difficult to imagine that a connection with God could satisfy our longings. This is a heartbreaking but real perspective.

TASTE AND SEE

Imagine a delicious plate of food being placed in front of you when you're extremely hungry. I immediately picture a juicy cheeseburger. Now in my state of hunger, would it be enough for me to simply smell that cheeseburger? Would it be enough to talk about how good that cheeseburger probably is? Of course not! To be satisfied by that burger, I would have to taste it to know that it is good. By actually eating the burger, not only would I know firsthand that it's actually delicious, but it's also the only way my hunger could be satisfied.

Psalm 34:8 says, "Taste and see how good the Lord is! The one who takes refuge in him is truly happy!" For many of us, it's laughable to think that spending time with Jesus could rival the satisfaction that we receive from some of our idols. That's because we have yet to "taste and see" that God is good.

When we actually stop and contemplate the goodness that God has exhibited to us, we taste and see. When we set other things aside and provide the Holy Spirit an uninterrupted venue to move in and speak to our hearts, we're able to taste and see. When we explore the Word of God with the expectation that God will actually speak to us through it, we're able to taste and see that God is good.

REAL VERSUS IMITATION

Speaking of tasting, there's usually a significant difference between tasting something that's real and tasting an imitation. For example, if you were a seafood lover and you were to try some delicious king crab legs, and someone offered you some imitation crab meat right after, there's no way that you would choose the imitation. Compared to the real thing, the imitation wouldn't even come close to satisfying. What's interesting, however, is that the more time that has passed between when we've tasted the real thing and when we're offered an imitation, the more likely we are to settle for the imitation.

We need to "taste" of the Lord daily so that we'll *never* be satisfied with an imitation. C. S. Lewis provides us with an insightful quotation that speaks directly to this issue:

> We are half-hearted creatures, fooling about with drink and sex and ambition when infinite joy is offered us, like an ignorant child who wants to go on making mud pies in a slum because he cannot imagine what is meant by the offer of a holiday at the sea. We are far too easily pleased.[5]

When we settle for the temporary satisfaction that comes from indulging in idol worship, it's like we're playing in mud rather than building sand castles. There is unspeakable joy and satisfaction that comes from the real, true, living God.

GOD GIVES GOOD GIFTS

Many people have a false belief that God's only dealings with us have to do with a desire to punish us for our wrong actions. We think of God like the Greek mythological character Zeus, who is ready to strike with a lightning bolt

---

5. From *The Weight of Glory, and Other Addresses*, by C.S. Lewis, in *The Essential C.S. Lewis*, edited by Lyle W. Dorsett, (Simon and Schuster, 1996); page 362.

when we act wrongly. But this isn't what the gospel tells us. Remember, *gospel* means "good news." If God's only desire were to crush us, that wouldn't be good news.

God is not only the one who can make us joyful but is the source of joy itself. Joy is a fruit of the Spirit, and it's through the Spirit of God that we find joy and satisfaction. God "wants all people to be saved and to come to a knowledge of the truth" (1 Timothy 2:4). And James 1:17 reminds us that:

> Every good gift, every perfect gift, comes from above. These gifts come down from the Father, the creator of the heavenly lights, in whose character there is no change at all.

As we lay down our idols and make ourselves available to be ministered to by the God who created us, we'll realize that God wants us to enjoy our special relationship.

GOD FILLS OUR NEEDS

Psalm 107:4-9 shows us a picture of God's ability to fulfill our longings:

> Some of the redeemed had wandered
>> into the desert, into the wasteland.
>> They couldn't find their way to a city or town.
> They were hungry and thirsty;
>> their lives were slipping away.
> So they cried out to the LORD
>> in their distress,
>> and God delivered them
>>> from their desperate circumstances.

God led them straight
　　to human habitation.
　Let them thank the Lord
　　for his faithful love
　　and his wondrous works for all people,
because God satisfied the one
　　who was parched with thirst,
　and he filled up the hungry
　　with good things!

Our longings for fulfillment are real, but our efforts to fill them with means other than God will always be futile. This is affirmed in Romans 8:22, when Paul talks about how all of creation groans and longs to be restored to the way God intended. The beauty of the verses in Psalm 107 is that we see that we are able to be satisfied when we cry out and allow God to be our remedy.

God promises in Revelation 21:5 to make all things new again, just like it was in the beginning of all creation. Paul tells us in Colossians 1:20 that God will reconcile, or "fix," all things in heaven and on earth. This is our hope. The beauty is that as we long for this ultimate restoration, we find satisfaction through Christ now, even in our broken and frail bodies.

HOPE IN COMMUNITY

At the beginning of every year, millions of people all across the country decide that it's time to do something about their personal fitness. Whether it's losing weight, getting in shape, or becoming healthy, many commitments are made toward accomplishing these goals. What I find interesting about these types of commitments is that if we keep them to ourselves, they're a lot more difficult to accomplish.

If I tell myself, "I'm going to eat healthier," and don't share my plan with anyone else; then as soon as temptation strikes, it will be easy for me to say, "I changed my mind," and eat whatever I want. It's a lot more difficult for me to forsake my commitment when I tell others what's going on, because they're going to challenge me when I want to throw in the towel. When they see me going astray, they'll stand with me and intervene.

This is also true as we journey toward laying down our idols. The people we're running with in the faith can be an encouragement by reminding us and challenging us about where we find our fulfillment.

YOU CAN DO IT

The belief that I could actually live in victory over idols eluded me for a while. I had the hardest time considering that life could move forward without the constant and strong magnetic pull of the idols that had stolen my affections over time. For so long, I would attempt to remove idols in my own strength and see failure over and over again.

I finally realized that it was Christ who had to be my redeemer and "idol crusher," and it was two verses in 2 Peter that began to help me to take root in a new journey toward victory:

> By his divine power the Lord has given us everything we need for life and godliness through the knowledge of the one who called us by his own honor and glory. Through his honor and glory he has given us his precious and wonderful promises, that you may share the divine nature and escape from the world's immorality that sinful craving produces. (2 Peter 1:3-4)

Talk about empowering! This passage articulates that we have everything for "life and godliness" through our knowledge of Jesus. We have what it takes to walk in victory but not through our own efforts. That comes only through the power of Jesus.

These verses assure us that we can do the very thing that we fear we can't. We can "escape from the world's immorality that sinful craving produces." So often we think that when temptation rears its ugly head in our lives, we won't have the ability to withstand it and do what is right.

It's true that we don't have the power on our own. But through the knowledge of the Lord, we do.

QUESTIONS

1. In Hebrews 4:1, what is the rest that believers can enter into?

2. What is the "good news" of Hebrews 4:2?

3. What is the connection between faith and entering God's rest (Hebrews 4:3)?

4. How do our stubborn hearts alienate us from God? How do we know whether our hearts are stubborn (Hebrews 4:7)?

5. What is the difference between God's *rest* and God's *sabbath rest* (Hebrews 4:8-10)?

6. In what ways is God's Word living and active (Hebrews 4:12)? Have you experienced this personally? If so, how?

7. Why is Jesus able to sympathize with our weaknesses (Hebrews 4:15)?

8. What is the "throne of favor" (Hebrews 4:16)? What does it mean to draw near to it with confidence? Why are we able to do this?

9. Why is community so important when we're trying to overcome sin?

10. How do we "share the divine nature" so that we can "escape from the world's immorality that sinful craving produces" (2 Peter 1:3-4)?

Check out Curtis Zackery's
other title in the Converge series!

Sharing the Gospel
9781426771569, Print
9781426771675, eBook

 Abingdon Press

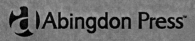

CPSIA information can be obtained at www.ICGtesting.com
Printed in the USA
LVOW12s0826150514

385625LV00005B/6/P

9 781426 795541